The Spiritual Journey to Somnath Jyotirlinga

The Spiritual Journey To Jyotirlingas, Volume 1

Rajesh Giri

Published by Rajesh Giri, 2023.

THE SPIRITUAL JOURNEY TO SOMNATH JYOTIRLINGA

First edition. March 13, 2023.

Copyright © 2023 Rajesh Giri.

ISBN: 979-8215698877

Written by Rajesh Giri.

Table of Contents

Dedication

This book is dedicated to all the followers of Sanatan Dharma and the devotees of Lord Shiva, who have a deep spiritual connection with Somnath Jyotirlinga. May this book serve as a guide to deepen your understanding and strengthen your faith in the divine power of Lord Shiva and the spiritual significance of Somnath Jyotirlinga.

Rajesh Giri
The Practical Success Coach

Legal Disclaimer

Preface

O Lord of Somnath Jyotirlinga divine,
Bless us with your grace that forever shine,
May we always find solace at your feet,
And from all troubles and sorrows be freed.
Your holy presence brings us peace and light,
May we always walk the path that is right,
Oh Somnath Jyotirlinga, hear our prayer,
And guide us towards the ultimate truth we seek with care.

Dear reader,

It is with great joy and devotion that I present to you **"The Spiritual Journey to Somnath Jyotirlinga"** This book is a humble attempt to guide you through the spiritual significance and rich history of Somnath Jyotirlinga, one of the most sacred and revered pilgrimage sites in India.

Somnath Temple, nestled in the picturesque town of Veraval in the Saurashtra region of Gujarat, is not just a temple but a symbol of devotion, resilience, and rebirth. Its history dates back to ancient times, and the temple has been destroyed and rebuilt multiple times, yet it stands tall today as a testament to the unshakeable faith of millions of devotees.

In this book, I shall take you on a journey to explore the myths, legends, and stories associated with Somnath Jyotirlinga, the architectural beauty of the temple, and the spiritual significance of performing puja at this sacred site. I shall also delve into the history of the temple and the role it played in the freedom struggle of India.

Moreover, I shall guide you through the best time to visit Somnath Jyotirlinga, how to reach the temple, and the accommodation options available for visitors. I shall also take a look at the local attractions near the temple and the festivals celebrated at Somnath.

I hope that this book will serve as a spiritual guide for all those who wish to embark on a journey of devotion and self-discovery. May the blessings of Lord Somnath be with you on this journey, and may you find peace, enlightenment, and inner strength in the holy abode of Somnath Jyotirlinga.

Rajesh Giri

The Practical Success Coach

The Spiritual Journey to Jyotirlinga

A journey to the Jyotirlinga,
A pilgrimage of heart and soul,
A path of love and devotion,
To reach the divine goal.
The lingam of light and power,
A symbol of the One Supreme,
The source of all creation,
The essence of every dream.
With each step taken forward,
The heart is filled with grace,
The mind is stilled to silence,
And the soul begins to pace.
The journey is not just physical,
But a spiritual awakening too,
The sacred bond with the Almighty,
Deepens with every view.
The sound of bells and chants,
Fills the air with sacred energy,
The fragrance of incense and flowers,
Envelops the soul with ecstasy.
The Jyotirlinga is not just a temple,
But a portal to the divine,
A sacred space to connect,
With the universal shrine.
May every step of the journey,
Be blessed with divine light,
May the Jyotirlinga fill your heart,
With love and blissful sight.

Somnath Jyotirlinga is one of the most revered pilgrimage sites in India, located in the Saurashtra region of Gujarat. The temple is dedicated to

Lord Shiva and is believed to be one of the twelve Jyotirlingas, which are considered to be the most sacred abodes of Lord Shiva.

The temple has a long and fascinating history, with various legends and stories associated with it. It has been destroyed and rebuilt several times over the centuries, yet it still stands as a symbol of resilience and rebirth. The temple's architectural beauty is also noteworthy, with intricate carvings and sculptures that showcase the skill and craftsmanship of ancient Indian artisans.

In this book, we will take a spiritual journey to Somnath Jyotirlinga and explore its significance in Hinduism. We will delve into the history of the temple, the mythology and legends associated with it, and its spiritual significance in modern times. We will also discuss the best time to visit, how to reach Somnath Jyotirlinga, and the accommodation options available for visitors.

Whether you are a devout follower of Lord Shiva or simply curious about the spiritual significance of this ancient temple, this book will provide you with a comprehensive guide to Somnath Jyotirlinga.

Chapter 1: Introduction to Somnath Jyotirlinga

Welcome to Somnath Jyotirlinga,
A temple of ancient lore,
A place of worship and devotion,
That the heart cannot ignore.
Here the lingam of Lord Shiva,
Stands tall and grand in view,
A symbol of divine power,
That we all look up to.
The sound of mantras and bhajans,
Fill the air with holy grace,
The fragrance of flowers and incense,
Envelops the soul with embrace.
The waves of the Arabian Sea,
Lash the shores with rhythmic sound,
The sky above is vast and clear,
A canvas where beauty is found.
In the land of Lord Krishna,
This holy site is revered,
The pilgrimage to Somnath,
Is a journey that we all should steer.
May the divine blessings of Lord Shiva,
Shower upon all who visit this shrine,
May the Somnath Jyotirlinga,
Be a beacon of light that forever shines.

Somnath Jyotirlinga is one of the twelve Jyotirlingas, which are considered to be the most sacred abodes of Lord Shiva. Located in the Prabhas Kshetra near Veraval in the Saurashtra region of Gujarat, India,

Somnath Jyotirlinga is a symbol of the ancient Indian civilization, its culture, and spirituality.

The Jyotirlinga is believed to have been originally built by Lord Chandra, the Moon God, at the behest of Lord Brahma. According to Hindu mythology, the Jyotirlinga is self-manifested and has a divine energy that can cure all ailments and bring peace and prosperity to those who visit it.

The temple has a rich history and has been destroyed and rebuilt several times over the centuries. It has been the target of numerous invaders, including Mahmud of Ghazni, who destroyed it in the 11th century. The temple was later rebuilt by King Bhimdev Solanki in the 12th century, only to be destroyed again by Allauddin Khilji in the 14th century. The temple was rebuilt once again in the 15th century, but was destroyed again by Mughal emperor Aurangzeb in the 17th century.

The temple was finally rebuilt in 1951, with the help of Sardar Vallabhbhai Patel, the first Home Minister of independent India. The current temple is a stunning example of Indian temple architecture and attracts visitors from all over the world.

The name 'Somnath' is derived from two Sanskrit words - 'som' meaning 'moon' and 'nath' meaning 'lord'. The Jyotirlinga is believed to be the embodiment of Lord Shiva as 'Someshwara', the Lord of the Moon. The temple is also associated with several mythological stories, including the legend of Lord Krishna, who is said to have left his mortal body at this site.

Today, Somnath Jyotirlinga is not just a place of worship, but a symbol of India's rich cultural heritage and spirituality. It is a testament to the resilience of the Indian people and their faith in the divine. Visitors to the temple are not just mesmerized by its beauty, but are also touched by its spiritual energy, which has the power to heal and rejuvenate the soul.

Chapter 2: History of Somnath Temple

The history of Somnath temple,
Is one of glory and might,
A tale of resilience and devotion,
That has withstood time's harsh bite.
Built by the great Soma dynasty,
This temple was a gem so rare,
A symbol of faith and worship,
That all could come and share.
From invasions by Mahmud of Ghazni,
To being destroyed by Aurangzeb's decree,
The temple faced destruction and ruin,
But its spirit remained free.
Each time it was rebuilt,
With more strength and devotion,
The faith of the devotees never wilted,
And kept the temple's flame in motion.
Today the Somnath temple stands,
As a testament to its past,
A place of worship and devotion,
That will forever last.
May the divine blessings of Lord Shiva,
Shower upon all who visit this shrine,
May the Somnath temple's history,
Be a source of inspiration for all time.

The history of the Somnath Temple is closely intertwined with the history of India. The temple has been destroyed and rebuilt several times over the centuries, each time as a testament to the resilience and determination of the Indian people.

The original temple is believed to have been built by Lord Chandra, the Moon God, as a symbol of his devotion to Lord Shiva. The temple was later renovated by King Vikramaditya, and again by King Bhoja of the Paramara dynasty. The temple was a major pilgrimage site for Hindus, attracting visitors from all over India.

In 1024 AD, the temple was attacked by Mahmud of Ghazni, a ruthless conqueror from Central Asia. Mahmud was known for his brutal raids on India, and he saw the temple as a symbol of Hindu pride and resistance. He ordered his soldiers to destroy the temple and loot its treasures.

The destruction of the Somnath Temple was a traumatic event for Hindus, and it sparked a wave of resistance against the invaders. The temple was rebuilt by King Bhimdev Solanki in the 12th century, and it became a symbol of Hindu defiance against foreign invaders.

In the 14th century, the temple was once again destroyed, this time by Allauddin Khilji, the Sultan of Delhi. Khilji was known for his brutal conquests and he saw the temple as a symbol of Hindu pride and resistance. The temple was rebuilt once again in the 15th century, but it was destroyed again by Mughal emperor Aurangzeb in the 17th century.

The temple remained in ruins for several centuries, until it was rebuilt in 1951 with the help of Sardar Vallabhbhai Patel, the first Home Minister of independent India. The current temple is a stunning example of Indian temple architecture and is considered to be one of the most important pilgrimage sites for Hindus.

The history of the Somnath Temple is a testament to the resilience and determination of the Indian people. Despite being destroyed several times, the temple has been rebuilt each time as a symbol of Hindu pride and defiance against foreign invaders. Today, the temple stands as a symbol of India's rich cultural heritage and spirituality, attracting visitors from all over the world.

Chapter 3: Mythological Significance of Somnath Jyotirlinga

The Somnath Jyotirlinga,
Has a mythological tale so grand,
Of Lord Shiva's divine presence,
In this sacred land.
Legend has it that Lord Krishna,
Worshipped the lingam here,
And that the Pandavas too,
Paid homage to it without fear.
It is said that the moon god,
Soma was cursed and lost his light,
But was restored by Lord Shiva,
When he prayed with all his might.
Thus the Jyotirlinga of Somnath,
Is a symbol of Shiva's divine grace,
A place of worship and devotion,
Where one can seek his face.
The temple's history is filled,
With tales of glory and might,
Of battles fought and won,
Against invaders that took flight.
May the divine blessings of Lord Shiva,
Shower upon all who visit this shrine,
May the Somnath Jyotirlinga's significance,
Fill our hearts with devotion divine.

According to Hindu mythology, Lord Shiva is the creator, preserver, and destroyer of the universe. He is one of the most revered deities in Hinduism and is worshipped in various forms across India. One of the most important forms of Lord Shiva is the Jyotirlinga, which represents the divine power of Shiva.

Somnath Jyotirlinga is one of the twelve Jyotirlingas in India and is considered to be one of the most important pilgrimage sites for Hindus. According to legend, the Jyotirlinga at Somnath was established by Lord Chandra, the Moon God, in honor of Lord Shiva.

The legend goes that Lord Chandra was cursed by his father-in-law, Sage Daksha, for being partial to his own sons and neglecting his daughters. The curse caused Lord Chandra to suffer from a disease that made him lose his luster and become weak. In his desperation, Lord Chandra prayed to Lord Shiva and performed penance at the site of the Somnath Jyotirlinga. Lord Shiva was pleased with Lord Chandra's devotion and appeared before him, curing him of his disease and restoring his luster.

Another legend associated with Somnath Jyotirlinga is that of King Bhimdev Solanki, who built the temple in the 12th century. According to the legend, King Bhimdev was a devotee of Lord Shiva and had a dream in which Lord Shiva appeared to him and instructed him to build a temple at the site of the Somnath Jyotirlinga.

The temple was built and became a major pilgrimage site for Hindus. The temple was attacked and destroyed several times over the centuries, but it was always rebuilt as a symbol of Hindu resilience and defiance against foreign invaders.

The mythological significance of Somnath Jyotirlinga lies in its association with Lord Shiva, one of the most important deities in Hinduism. The Jyotirlinga represents the divine power of Shiva and is believed to have the power to grant wishes and cure diseases. The legends associated with Somnath Jyotirlinga speak of the power of devotion and the importance of preserving one's cultural heritage. Today, the temple continues to attract visitors from all over the world, who come to seek the blessings of Lord Shiva and experience the rich cultural heritage of India.

Chapter 4: Architectural Beauty of Somnath Temple

The Somnath temple's architectural beauty,
Is a sight to behold and admire,
A marvel of ancient Indian craftsmanship,
That fills the heart with desire.
The temple's soaring spire,
Reaches up towards the sky,
Its intricate carvings and sculptures,
Are a feast for the eye.
The temple's inner sanctum,
Houses the Jyotirlinga with care,
Its ornate decorations and paintings,
Are a sight so rare.
The sound of the temple bells,
And the aroma of incense and flowers,
Creates an ambiance so divine,
That one forgets all worldly powers.
The temple's courtyards and halls,
Are adorned with stunning art,
Depicting tales of ancient lore,
That touch the soul and heart.
May the divine blessings of Lord Shiva,
Shower upon all who visit this shrine,
May the Somnath temple's architectural beauty,
Enrapture our senses for all time.

The Somnath Temple is an architectural marvel and is considered to be one of the most beautiful and intricate temples in India. The temple has undergone several renovations and restorations over the centuries, but its beauty and grandeur have remained intact.

The temple is built in the Chalukya style of architecture and is made of red sandstone. The temple complex is spread over an area of 20 acres and includes several smaller shrines and temples.

The main temple is built on a raised platform and is surrounded by a large courtyard. The temple has a tall shikara, or tower, that rises to a height of 150 feet. The tower is adorned with intricate carvings of gods and goddesses, animals, and mythological scenes.

The entrance to the temple is through a large gate known as the Mahadwara. The gate is decorated with intricate carvings of gods and goddesses and leads to the main courtyard.

The main temple is a circular structure with a domed roof. The dome is supported by 56 pillars, each of which is intricately carved with scenes from Hindu mythology. The inner sanctum houses the lingam, or the symbol of Lord Shiva.

The temple also has a large sabha mandap, or assembly hall, which is supported by 18 pillars. The hall is decorated with intricate carvings of gods and goddesses and is used for various ceremonies and rituals.

The temple complex also includes several smaller shrines and temples dedicated to various gods and goddesses. These shrines are decorated with intricate carvings and paintings and are considered to be some of the finest examples of Indian art and architecture.

The architectural beauty of the Somnath Temple is a testament to the skill and craftsmanship of the artisans and architects of ancient India. The temple is a living monument to the rich cultural heritage of India and continues to inspire awe and admiration among visitors from all over the world.

Chapter 5: Significance of Performing Puja at Somnath Temple

Performing puja at Somnath temple,
Is a spiritual experience so pure,
A divine connection with Lord Shiva,
That will forever endure.
The rituals and offerings made,
In this sacred space so divine,
Are a way to express devotion,
And seek blessings that shine.
The sound of the priests chanting mantras,
And the fragrance of flowers and incense,
Creates an ambiance of holiness,
That fills the heart with intense.
The act of circumambulating the temple,
And seeking the Lord's holy sight,
Is a way to cleanse the mind and soul,
And bask in divine light.
May the blessings of Lord Shiva,
Shower upon all who perform puja here,
May the Somnath temple be a source of,
Spiritual awakening that's always near.

The Somnath Temple is one of the most sacred shrines in India and is considered to be a place of great spiritual significance. Thousands of devotees visit the temple every year to seek the blessings of Lord Shiva and to perform puja, or worship.

Performing puja at the Somnath Temple is believed to bring immense spiritual benefits to the devotee. It is believed that the lingam, or the symbol of Lord Shiva, has a powerful aura that can purify the mind and body of the devotee.

The puja ceremony involves the offering of various items to the lingam, such as flowers, fruits, and sweets. The devotee also offers prayers and chants mantras to invoke the blessings of Lord Shiva.

Performing puja at the Somnath Temple is also believed to bring good luck and prosperity to the devotee. It is said that the blessings of Lord Shiva can remove all obstacles and difficulties from one's life and bring peace and happiness.

In addition to the spiritual benefits, performing puja at the Somnath Temple is also a way to connect with the rich cultural heritage of India. The temple is a living monument to the art, architecture, and spiritual traditions of ancient India and is a source of inspiration for people from all walks of life.

Devotees also perform special pujas on important occasions such as Maha Shivaratri and Shravan Maas, which are considered to be particularly auspicious for seeking the blessings of Lord Shiva.

Overall, performing puja at the Somnath Temple is a deeply fulfilling and enriching experience that can bring immense spiritual and cultural benefits to the devotee.

Chapter 6: Importance of Somnath Temple in Hinduism

The Somnath temple's importance,
In Hinduism is great and vast,
It is one of the twelve Jyotirlingas,
That devotees hold steadfast.
The temple is a symbol of faith,
And of the triumph of devotion,
It has withstood the tests of time,
And has remained a source of emotion.
The temple's history and mythology,
Are woven into the fabric of Hindu lore,
And its significance in the religion,
Is something that devotees adore.
The temple's sanctity and divine aura,
Are a source of inspiration for all,
And the pilgrimage to Somnath,
Is a journey that one should not stall.
May the blessings of Lord Shiva,
Shower upon all who visit this shrine,
May the Somnath temple's importance,
Remain forever divine and fine.

The Somnath Temple holds great importance in Hinduism and is considered to be one of the most sacred places of worship for Hindus. The temple is dedicated to Lord Shiva and is believed to be the first of the twelve Jyotirlingas, which are considered to be the most revered shrines of Lord Shiva.

According to Hindu mythology, Lord Brahma, the creator of the universe, had performed a yagna, or a sacrificial offering, at the site where the temple now stands. It is believed that the lingam, or the symbol of

Lord Shiva, appeared during the yagna, and Lord Brahma established the temple to honor Lord Shiva.

The temple has a rich and fascinating history and has been destroyed and rebuilt several times over the centuries. It has been attacked by invaders and rulers from different parts of India and has been rebuilt each time as a symbol of the indomitable spirit of the Indian people.

Apart from its historical significance, the Somnath Temple also holds great spiritual importance for Hindus. It is believed that a visit to the temple and the darshan, or the sight, of the lingam can bring immense spiritual benefits to the devotee.

The temple is also associated with several important Hindu festivals and is a hub of activity during these occasions. Maha Shivaratri, which is celebrated in honor of Lord Shiva, is one of the most important festivals celebrated at the Somnath Temple.

Overall, the Somnath Temple is a symbol of the rich cultural heritage and spiritual traditions of India. It is a testament to the enduring faith and devotion of Hindus and serves as a source of inspiration for people from all walks of life.

Chapter 7: Legends and Stories Associated with Somnath Jyotirlinga

The Somnath Jyotirlinga,
Is steeped in legends and tales,
Of ancient Hindu mythology,
That still mystifies and enthralls.
It is said that Lord Krishna,
Built the original temple with care,
And the Pandavas too,
Paid homage to it without fear.
Legend has it that the moon god,
Soma was cursed and lost his light,
But was restored by Lord Shiva,
When he prayed with all his might.
The temple's history is filled,
With tales of glory and might,
Of battles fought and won,
Against invaders that took flight.
The temple's sanctum sanctorum,
Is where the Jyotirlinga resides,
And the act of seeking its darshan,
Is something that one should abide.
May the blessings of Lord Shiva,
Shower upon all who know these tales,
May the legends of Somnath Jyotirlinga,
Enrich our souls and lift our sails.

The Somnath Jyotirlinga is surrounded by several legends and stories that have been passed down through generations. These legends and stories not only add to the mystical aura of the temple but also provide a deeper understanding of the spiritual significance of the shrine.

One of the most popular legends associated with the temple is that of the demon king Ravana. According to the legend, Ravana had performed intense penance to please Lord Shiva and had obtained the powerful lingam from the lord as a reward. However, on his journey back to Lanka, the demon king had to take a break and had entrusted the lingam to a local shepherd boy for safekeeping. When Ravana returned, he was enraged to find that the boy had placed the lingam on the ground and had disappeared. Despite his best efforts, Ravana was unable to lift the lingam, and it became firmly rooted in the ground, becoming the Somnath Jyotirlinga.

Another popular legend associated with the temple is that of the moon god, Chandra. According to the legend, Chandra had been cursed by his father-in-law, Daksha, and had lost his luster and radiance. Seeking redemption, Chandra had performed penance at the Somnath Temple and had been blessed by Lord Shiva, who had restored his radiance.

Yet another legend associated with the temple is that of Lord Krishna. According to the legend, Lord Krishna had visited the Somnath Temple during his lifetime and had been impressed by its spiritual energy. He had performed aarti, or the ritual of waving a lamp in front of the deity, at the temple, and had prayed for the prosperity and well-being of his people.

These legends and stories associated with the Somnath Jyotirlinga are an integral part of the temple's history and spirituality. They provide a glimpse into the rich cultural heritage of India and serve as a source of inspiration and devotion for millions of Hindus around the world.

Chapter 8: Somnath Temple as a Symbol of Resilience and Rebirth

The Somnath temple stands,
As a symbol of resilience and rebirth,
For despite being destroyed and rebuilt,
Its spirit remains unscathed and mirth.
The temple's history is rife,
With tales of invasion and destruction,
But each time it has risen,
Like a phoenix from the eruption.
The temple's strength lies,
In its devotees' unflinching faith,
For they have kept the flame burning,
Through centuries of strife and wraith.
The temple's glory and grandeur,
Are a testament to its fortitude,
And its significance in Hinduism,
Is something that cannot be subdued.
May the Somnath temple's resilience,
Inspire us in our daily lives,
To weather the storms of existence,
And emerge triumphant, like the temple that thrives.

The Somnath Temple has been destroyed and rebuilt several times throughout history, making it a symbol of resilience and rebirth. The temple has been the target of numerous invasions and attacks, including those by foreign invaders such as Mahmud of Ghazni, who destroyed the temple in the 11th century and looted its treasures.

Despite these attacks, the temple has always risen from the ashes, rebuilt and restored by devotees who consider it to be one of the holiest sites in the country. The resilience of the Somnath Temple has become a symbol of hope and perseverance for people all over the world.

The rebuilding of the temple has been a collaborative effort of people from different faiths and cultures. It is said that after the temple was destroyed by Mahmud of Ghazni, a wealthy merchant named Bhima donated all of his wealth to rebuild the temple. It was also rebuilt by the Chaulukya dynasty and the Yadava dynasty.

The temple was again destroyed by the Mughal emperor Aurangzeb in the 17th century, but it was rebuilt once again by the Peshwa rulers of Maharashtra. The current temple was built in 1951 by Sardar Vallabhbhai Patel, India's first deputy Prime Minister, after India gained independence from British rule.

The Somnath Temple's ability to survive and rise from the ashes is a testament to the power of faith, hope, and determination. It has become a symbol of the resilience of the Indian people, who have faced numerous challenges throughout their history but have always found a way to rebuild and move forward.

The temple's story serves as an inspiration for people all over the world who face adversity and challenges in their lives. It teaches us that no matter how many times we fall, we must always get up and keep moving forward, with faith and determination in our hearts. The Somnath Temple's story is a reminder that there is always hope, and that even in the darkest of times, there is a light that can guide us towards a brighter tomorrow.

Chapter 9: Spiritual Significance of Somnath Jyotirlinga in Modern Times

In these modern times,
The Somnath Jyotirlinga's spiritual significance,
Is as relevant as it was in ancient times,
For it offers a way to find deliverance.
The temple's sanctity and serenity,
Is a respite from the chaos of daily life,
And its aura of divinity,
Can soothe the soul's strife.
The act of seeking the Lord's blessings,
Through prayers and offerings made,
Can bring about a transformation,
In the way one thinks and behaves.
The temple's Jyotirlinga is a symbol,
Of the infinite and eternal nature of Shiva,
And seeking its darshan can lead one,
To a state of bliss and tranquility that's pure.
May the Somnath Jyotirlinga's spiritual significance,
Guide us on our spiritual journey each day,
And may it serve as a beacon of light,
That illuminates our path along the way.

The Somnath Temple remains an important pilgrimage site for Hindus in modern times, with thousands of devotees visiting every year. The spiritual significance of the temple lies in the belief that it is one of the twelve Jyotirlingas or pillars of light, which are believed to represent the divine form of Lord Shiva.

According to Hindu mythology, Lord Shiva is believed to have manifested in the form of a Jyotirlinga, which represents his infinite nature and power. The Somnath Jyotirlinga is believed to have been established by Lord Brahma himself, and it is said that worshipping at this temple can bestow great blessings and spiritual benefits upon the devotees.

The temple is also associated with several important Hindu festivals such as Maha Shivratri, Navratri, and Diwali. During these festivals, the temple is decorated with lights, flowers, and colorful decorations, and devotees gather to offer prayers and seek the blessings of Lord Shiva.

Apart from its religious significance, the Somnath Temple also has great cultural and historical significance. The temple's architecture and design reflect the influences of various dynasties that have ruled over the region, including the Chaulukya, Yadava, and Peshwa dynasties.

The temple is also located in a beautiful coastal area, which adds to its charm and attracts tourists from all over the world. The surrounding area is known for its scenic beauty, and visitors can enjoy the picturesque views of the Arabian Sea and nearby beaches.

In modern times, the Somnath Temple has become a symbol of India's rich cultural and religious heritage. It is a testament to the country's enduring spiritual traditions and the resilience of its people. The temple continues to inspire and attract devotees and visitors from all over the world, who seek to experience its spiritual and cultural significance firsthand.

Chapter 10: Best Time to Visit Somnath Jyotirlinga

The best time to visit Somnath Jyotirlinga,
Is when the air is filled with a cool breeze,
And the sky is a clear blue,
And the sun's rays caress the trees.
During the winter months,
From October to February,
The weather is pleasant and mild,
And the temple's ambiance is cheery.
The festival of Shivratri,
Is another ideal time to visit,
For the temple's festivities,
Are a sight that's sure to elicit.
The temple's beauty and grandeur,
Are a sight to behold year-round,
But visiting during these times,
Is sure to leave one spellbound.
May the Somnath Jyotirlinga's divine aura,
Guide us to the temple with ease,
And may our visit there,
Bring us peace and spiritual release.

The Somnath Jyotirlinga is one of the most revered and ancient temples in India, and attracts visitors from all over the world. The temple is open throughout the year, but the best time to visit Somnath Jyotirlinga depends on various factors such as weather, festivals, and personal preferences.

The ideal time to visit Somnath Jyotirlinga is during the winter season, from November to February, when the weather is cool and pleasant. The temperature during this time ranges between 10°C to

25°C, making it an ideal time for sightseeing and exploring the temple and its surroundings. The days are pleasant, and the nights are cold, so visitors are advised to carry warm clothing.

Another good time to visit Somnath Jyotirlinga is during the monsoon season, from June to September, when the region receives moderate to heavy rainfall. The lush green surroundings and the pleasant weather make it an ideal time for nature lovers and photographers. However, it is advisable to check the weather forecast before planning a trip during this season as heavy rainfall can lead to roadblocks and disruptions.

The summer season, from March to May, is not an ideal time to visit Somnath Jyotirlinga as the temperature can soar up to 40°C, making it difficult to explore the temple and its surroundings. However, for those who do not mind the heat, this season can offer cheaper accommodations and fewer crowds.

The temple is also especially crowded during festivals such as Maha Shivratri, Navratri, and Diwali. These festivals attract thousands of devotees who come to offer their prayers and seek the blessings of Lord Shiva. Visitors who want to experience the festive atmosphere and witness the grand celebrations should plan their visit accordingly.

In conclusion, the best time to visit Somnath Jyotirlinga depends on personal preferences and various factors such as weather and festivals. Visitors should plan their trip accordingly and carry appropriate clothing and gear to make the most of their visit.

Chapter 11: How to Reach Somnath Jyotirlinga

To reach Somnath Jyotirlinga,
There are many ways to embark,
But the journey itself,
Is a way to ignite the spiritual spark.
By air, one can fly,
To Diu or Porbandar,
And from there, take a cab or bus,
To reach the temple that's grander.
By rail, the nearest station,
Is Veraval, just a few kilometers away,
And from there, one can take a taxi,
To reach the temple and start to pray.
By road, one can drive,
From nearby cities and towns,
And the road trip itself,
Can be an adventure that astounds.
Whatever way one chooses,
To reach the Somnath Jyotirlinga,
The journey is as important,
As the destination, it's worth remembering.
May the Lord's blessings guide us,
On the journey to the temple of light,
And may our visit to Somnath,
Be a source of spiritual delight.

Somnath Jyotirlinga is located in the western Indian state of Gujarat, near the town of Veraval in the Saurashtra region. It is well-connected by various modes of transportation, making it easily accessible for devotees and tourists.

By Air: The nearest airport to Somnath is Keshod airport, which is located about 55 km away. Another option is the Diu airport, which is about 80 km away. Both airports have regular flights to major Indian cities like Mumbai, Ahmedabad, and Jaipur. From the airport, you can hire a taxi or take a bus to reach Somnath.

By Train: Veraval railway station, located about 6 km from Somnath, is the nearest railway station. It is well-connected to major cities like Ahmedabad, Rajkot, Mumbai, and Delhi. From the station, you can take a taxi or an auto-rickshaw to reach the temple.

By Road: Somnath is well-connected by road to major cities in Gujarat and other nearby states. State-run buses and private buses ply regularly from cities like Ahmedabad, Rajkot, Junagadh, and Dwarka. You can also hire a taxi or a private car to reach Somnath.

Once you reach Somnath, you can hire a taxi or an auto-rickshaw to visit the temple and explore the surrounding areas. It is advisable to plan your trip in advance and make bookings for travel and accommodation, especially during peak tourist seasons.

Chapter 12: Accommodation Options for Visitors to Somnath Temple

For visitors to Somnath Temple,
Accommodation options abound,
From luxurious hotels to budget stays,
There's a place for every pilgrim to be found.
The temple's own guest house,
Offers comfortable rooms and amenities,
And its proximity to the temple,
Makes it a popular choice for many.
There are also many hotels,
In and around the temple town,
Offering a range of services,
From basic to high-end crown.
For those on a tight budget,
There are many guest houses and lodges,
That offer affordable options,
To rest and rejuvenate one's bodges.
No matter where one chooses to stay,
The focus should be on the divine,
And the opportunity to seek the Lord's blessings,
At the Somnath Jyotirlinga shrine.
May our stay be peaceful and comfortable,
And may our focus remain on the divine,
As we seek the Lord's blessings,
At the Somnath Temple that's sublime.

Somnath Jyotirlinga is a popular pilgrimage destination for Hindus, and attracts thousands of visitors every year. There are several accommodation options available for those visiting the temple, ranging from budget-friendly guesthouses to luxury hotels.

1. Somnath Trust Guesthouses: The Somnath Trust offers guesthouses near the temple, which are reasonably priced and clean. They have different types of rooms available to suit different budgets, and provide basic amenities like air conditioning, television, and attached bathrooms.
2. State Tourism Department Guesthouses: The Gujarat State Tourism Department also has guesthouses near the temple, which are reasonably priced and clean. They have different types of rooms available to suit different budgets, and provide basic amenities like air conditioning, television, and attached bathrooms.
3. Private Hotels and Resorts: There are several private hotels and resorts located in and around Somnath, which cater to different budgets and preferences. These hotels provide a range of facilities and services, including swimming pools, restaurants, and spas.
4. Dharamshalas: There are several dharamshalas located near the temple, which provide basic accommodation at very low prices. These are usually run by charitable trusts and provide dormitory-style accommodation, with shared bathrooms.
5. Camping: For those who prefer to be close to nature, there are several camping options available near Somnath. You can pitch a tent or rent a pre-set tent at one of the many campsites located in the vicinity of the temple.

It is advisable to book your accommodation in advance, especially during peak tourist seasons like Diwali and Navratri. You can book your accommodation online or through a travel agent.

Chapter 13: Local Attractions Near Somnath Temple

Near Somnath Temple, there are sights to see,
That add to the experience of the pilgrimage spree,
From historical monuments to scenic spots,
There's much to explore, in this beautiful spot.
The Prabhas Patan Museum,
Is a treasure trove of history and art,
With exhibits that showcase the region's past,
And leave a lasting impression on the heart.
The Bhalka Tirtha, a holy site,
Is where Lord Krishna took his final flight,
And its spiritual significance,
Is a beacon of divine light.
The beautiful beaches of Somnath,
Are a sight to behold and admire,
With their pristine waters and golden sands,
They offer a calming and serene desire.
Gir National Park, a wildlife sanctuary,
Is home to the majestic Asiatic lion,
And the chance to see this regal beast,
Is a truly unforgettable boon.
No matter what one chooses to see,
The Somnath Jyotirlinga remains the central key,
For it is the divine light that guides us all,
And the spiritual center that we heed to call.
May our visit to Somnath,
Be an enriching and uplifting spree,
And may we leave with blessings galore,
From this land of divinity.

In addition to the spiritual significance of Somnath Jyotirlinga, there are several other attractions near the temple that visitors can explore during their trip to Saurashtra. Here are some of the most popular local attractions:

1. Triveni Sangam: This is the confluence of three holy rivers, namely Hiran, Kapila and Saraswati, which is located near the Somnath Temple. It is considered an auspicious place for performing rituals and is also a popular picnic spot.
2. Bhalka Tirtha: According to Hindu mythology, Lord Krishna was accidentally shot by an arrow in the foot while resting under a peepal tree at this spot. Bhalka Tirtha is now a temple built in memory of Lord Krishna and is located close to the Somnath Temple.
3. Geeta Mandir: This temple is dedicated to the teachings of the Bhagavad Gita, one of the most important Hindu scriptures. The temple is adorned with beautiful paintings depicting the teachings of the Bhagavad Gita.
4. Junagadh: This is a historic city located near Somnath and is home to several attractions such as the Uparkot Fort, Mahabat Maqbara and the Junagadh Zoo.
5. Gir National Park: This is a famous wildlife sanctuary located near Somnath and is home to the majestic Asiatic lions. Visitors can go on a jungle safari to spot these magnificent creatures and other wildlife such as leopards, hyenas, and various species of birds.
6. Chorwad Beach: This is a scenic beach located near Somnath and is a popular spot for relaxing and enjoying the sunset. Visitors can also indulge in water sports such as jet skiing and parasailing.
7. Veraval Port: This is a busy fishing port located near Somnath and is home to several fishing communities. Visitors can watch the fishermen bring in their catch of the day and explore the

local fish market.

These local attractions add to the overall experience of visiting Somnath Jyotirlinga and provide visitors with a glimpse into the rich cultural heritage of Saurashtra.

Chapter 14: Festivals Celebrated at Somnath Temple

At the Somnath Temple, the air is abuzz,
With festivities that fill hearts with love,
From grand processions to sacred rituals,
The celebrations are truly divine and spiritual.
Mahashivratri, a grand festival,
Celebrates Lord Shiva in all his glory,
With offerings of flowers and sweets,
And prayers that echo in every story.
Ganesh Chaturthi, a joyous time,
Honors Lord Ganesha, the remover of obstacles,
With colorful decorations and lively processions,
The spirit of the festival is truly remarkable.
Janmashtami, the birth of Lord Krishna,
Is celebrated with great devotion and zeal,
With music, dance and elaborate feasts,
The festivities are truly surreal.
Navratri, a nine-day celebration,
Honors the divine feminine power,
With fasting, prayers and vibrant dances,
It's a time to unite and flower.
No matter which festival one celebrates,
The Somnath Temple offers a space,
To connect with the divine and feel blessed,
In an atmosphere that's filled with grace.
May these festivals bring us closer,
To the divine and our spiritual nature,
And may we continue to celebrate,
The Somnath Temple with utmost rapture.

Somnath Temple is not only a place of spiritual significance but also a cultural hub. The temple celebrates many festivals throughout the year, each with its unique customs and rituals. These festivals attract a large number of devotees and tourists to the temple, making it a bustling center of activity.

1. Mahashivratri: Mahashivratri is one of the most important festivals celebrated at Somnath Temple. It falls on the 14th day of the dark fortnight in the month of Phalguna (February/March) according to the Hindu calendar. On this day, devotees fast and offer prayers to Lord Shiva, the presiding deity of the temple. The festival is celebrated with great fervor and devotion, and many cultural programs and events are organized to mark the occasion.

2. Kartik Purnima: Kartik Purnima is another important festival celebrated at Somnath Temple. It falls on the full moon day in the month of Kartik (October/November) according to the Hindu calendar. On this day, devotees take a holy dip in the ocean near the temple and offer prayers to Lord Shiva. The festival is celebrated with the lighting of diyas (lamps) and the offering of sweets to the deity.

3. Diwali: Diwali, the festival of lights, is also celebrated at Somnath Temple with great enthusiasm. The festival falls in the month of October/November, according to the Hindu calendar. On this day, the temple is decorated with lights and flowers, and devotees offer prayers to Lord Shiva. The festival is also marked by the lighting of diyas and the distribution of sweets among devotees.

4. Holi: Holi, the festival of colors, is another popular festival celebrated at Somnath Temple. The festival falls in the month of March, according to the Hindu calendar. On this day, devotees throw colored powder and water at each other, signifying the triumph of good over evil. The festival is

celebrated with great joy and enthusiasm, and many cultural programs and events are organized to mark the occasion.

5. Janmashtami: Janmashtami, the birth anniversary of Lord Krishna, is also celebrated at Somnath Temple. The festival falls in the month of August/September, according to the Hindu calendar. On this day, devotees offer prayers to Lord Krishna and perform various rituals and customs to mark the occasion. The festival is celebrated with great devotion and enthusiasm, and many cultural programs and events are organized to mark the occasion.

6. Navratri: Navratri, a nine-day festival dedicated to the worship of the divine feminine, is also celebrated at Somnath Temple. The festival falls in the month of September/October, according to the Hindu calendar. On this day, devotees offer prayers to the nine forms of the goddess Durga, and perform various rituals and customs to mark the occasion. The festival is celebrated with great fervor and devotion, and many cultural programs and events are organized to mark the occasion.

In addition to these festivals, other important festivals celebrated at Somnath Temple include Gudi Padwa, Makar Sankranti, and Dussehra. Each festival is marked by its unique customs and rituals, and offers a glimpse into the rich cultural heritage of India.

Chapter 15: Conclusion and Final Thoughts on Somnath Jyotirlinga

In the heart of Gujarat, by the Arabian Sea,
Stands the Somnath Temple, a divine sanctuary,
With its ancient history and spiritual might,
It's a place where faith and devotion unite.
From the myths and legends that surround,
To the architectural beauty that astounds,
The Somnath Jyotirlinga is a sight to behold,
And a pilgrimage that's worth the journey and the bold.
For those who seek the divine light,
And wish to connect with it with all their might,
The Somnath Temple offers a sacred space,
Where one can feel the divine grace.
It's a symbol of resilience and rebirth,
And a place where one can find true worth,
A reminder of our spiritual nature,
And a beacon of hope and inner nurture.
May the blessings of Somnath Jyotirlinga,
Guide us through our journey in life,
And may we continue to seek and connect,
With the divine light that shines so bright.

Somnath Jyotirlinga is a revered temple and one of the most important pilgrimage sites for Hindus. With its rich history, mythological significance, and spiritual energy, the temple attracts millions of devotees every year. The temple is not only a symbol of Hinduism but also a symbol of resilience and rebirth.

Throughout this book, we have explored the history and mythological significance of the temple, the architectural beauty, and the spiritual importance of performing puja at the temple. We have also discussed the legends and stories associated with the temple and its significance in modern times.

Somnath Temple is not just a religious site, it is also a tourist attraction. Visitors can enjoy the beautiful surroundings and local attractions in the area. The festivals celebrated at the temple are also a unique experience, providing an opportunity to witness the colorful and vibrant culture of Gujarat.

The best time to visit Somnath Temple is during the winter months between November and February, when the weather is pleasant and cool. Visitors can reach the temple by road, train, or air, and there are several accommodation options available to suit every budget.

In conclusion, Somnath Jyotirlinga is a place of great importance to Hindus and a must-visit destination for anyone interested in exploring the rich cultural heritage of India. Its significance in history, myth, and spirituality is matched only by the awe-inspiring beauty of its architecture and the spiritual energy that emanates from the temple. A visit to Somnath Jyotirlinga is a journey of the soul and a truly unforgettable experience.

Read Some Stories Associated With The Somnath Jyotirlinga

Story of King Chandradev

Once upon a time, there was a pious and devout king named Chandradev who ruled the kingdom of Saurashtra. He was a great devotee of Lord Shiva and used to perform daily puja in his palace. However, he had always dreamt of visiting the Somnath Jyotirlinga and offering his prayers to the Lord in person.

One day, he set out on a journey to Somnath temple with his ministers and soldiers. The journey was long and arduous, but the king's devotion and determination kept him going. When they finally reached the temple, they were awed by its grandeur and beauty. The king was overwhelmed with emotion and fell to his knees in front of the lingam.

As he closed his eyes to offer his prayers, he suddenly heard a voice that said, "Oh Chandradev, I am pleased with your devotion and your long journey to reach me. I will grant you a boon, ask for anything you desire."

The king was overjoyed and thanked the Lord for his grace. He then requested the Lord to bless him with a son who would be a great ruler and a true devotee of Lord Shiva. Pleased with the king's devotion, Lord Shiva blessed him with a son who grew up to be a just and righteous ruler, who continued to spread the message of Lord Shiva's teachings throughout the kingdom.

From that day on, the Somnath Jyotirlinga became an important pilgrimage site for the people of Saurashtra, and the story of King Chandradev's devotion and the Lord's blessings continued to inspire generations of devotees.

The Pandavas' Divine Intervention

During their pilgrimage, the Pandavas arrived at the gates of Somnath Jyotirlinga, where they hoped to offer their prayers to Lord Shiva. However, they were met by a fierce demon named Bana, who denied them entry into the temple.

Determined to fulfill their mission, the Pandavas engaged in a fierce battle with Bana and his army. Despite their valiant efforts, the Pandavas found themselves overwhelmed by the demon's dark powers.

Just when all seemed lost, Lord Shiva appeared before them, his radiant form illuminating the battlefield. Moved by the Pandavas' devotion to him, Lord Shiva blessed them with victory and vanquished Bana and his army.

With the demon defeated and the temple now open, the Pandavas offered their prayers to Lord Shiva, grateful for his divine intervention. From that day on, it is said that the Pandavas' devotion to Lord Shiva at Somnath Jyotirlinga earned them his blessings and protection.

As they continued on their pilgrimage, the Pandavas reflected on the power of faith and the importance of standing up for what is right, no matter the obstacles they may face.

The Moon's Redemption

The Moon (Chandra) was a proud and powerful deity, married to the 27 daughters of Daksha Prajapati, a powerful son of Lord Brahma. Amongst his wives, Chandra favored Rohini, showering her with more attention and affection than the others. This led to resentment and anger amongst his other wives, who complained to their father about Chandra's unfair treatment.

Daksha, furious at Chandra's behavior, decided to teach him a lesson. He cursed Chandra with a disease that caused him to gradually lose his light. As the days passed, Chandra's form grew weaker, and his light dimmed until he was nothing more than a mere shadow of his former self.

Desperate to save himself, Chandra sought the advice of the other gods, who advised him to seek Lord Shiva's forgiveness and blessings. Chandra traveled to Somnath Jyotirlinga, a holy shrine dedicated to Lord Shiva, and offered his prayers to the Lord.

Moved by Chandra's devotion, Lord Shiva appeared before him, and Chandra pleaded for his forgiveness and help. Lord Shiva was pleased with Chandra's repentance and blessed him, curing him of his disease and restoring his light.

Chandra was overjoyed and grateful for Lord Shiva's mercy, and he promised to always honor and worship the Lord. Since that day, Lord Shiva has resided at Somnath Jyotirlinga, blessing all who visit the temple with his divine presence and protection.

Chandra learned a valuable lesson that day - that no one is above the laws of the universe and that pride and arrogance can lead to downfall. Through his redemption and Lord Shiva's blessings, Chandra was able to regain his light and return to his former glory, humbled and grateful for the Lord's mercy.

The Story of Ravana's Attraction to Somnath Jyotirlinga

According to the Hindu epic Ramayana, the demon king Ravana was a devout worshipper of Lord Shiva and had ten heads. Ravana was eager to have the divine power of Lord Shiva and therefore, he undertook a tough penance to please Lord Shiva. Pleased with his devotion, Lord Shiva appeared before Ravana and asked him to ask for a boon.

Ravana, being a wise man, asked for the power of immortality but Lord Shiva refused and instead, gave him a Shivlinga to worship and said that if he installed it at a place and performed his daily rituals, he would be invincible.

Ravana was pleased and decided to carry the Shivlinga to his capital Lanka. However, the gods were not happy with this and requested Lord Vishnu to intervene. Lord Vishnu took the form of a Brahmin and offered to carry the Shivlinga to Lanka. Ravana agreed but warned the Brahmin that he would not place the Shivlinga on the ground until he reached Lanka.

As he travelled towards Lanka, Ravana felt the urge to answer the call of nature and asked a boy standing nearby to hold the Shivlinga for a short while. However, the boy placed the Shivlinga on the ground and disappeared. The Shivlinga got embedded into the earth and Ravana was unable to move it.

Thus, the Shivlinga came to be known as Somnath Jyotirlinga and the temple was built around it.

The Story of King Bhimdev's Devotion to Somnath Jyotirlinga

King Bhimdev of the Solanki dynasty was a devout worshipper of Lord Shiva and built the temple of Somnath Jyotirlinga in the 11th century. He believed that the temple should be built in such a way that it could withstand all natural calamities and external invasions.

To ensure the same, he used gold and precious stones to build the temple and installed a magnificent idol of Lord Shiva in the temple. He also built a large reservoir to provide water to the temple and its devotees.

The temple became famous all over India for its grandeur and became a major pilgrimage center for devotees of Lord Shiva. However, during the invasion of Mahmud Ghazni in the 11th century, the temple was destroyed and looted.

Despite the destruction of the temple, the devotees of Lord Shiva continued to visit the site and rebuilt the temple several times over the years. The temple stands today as a symbol of the devotion of the followers of Lord Shiva and their resilience in the face of adversity.

The Power of Devotion

King Chandrasena of the Yadava dynasty was a devout follower of Lord Shiva, and he longed to build a grand temple dedicated to the Lord. However, he lacked the necessary resources to fulfill his dream. One night, Lord Shiva appeared to him in a dream and told him to perform a yagna at the Somnath Jyotirlinga.

The king, eager to follow Lord Shiva's instructions, arranged for the yagna to be performed at the holy site. He and his priests prayed and offered sacrifices to the Lord with utmost devotion. The yagna lasted for days, and the king's faith never faltered.

As the yagna came to an end, King Chandrasena was surprised to discover a large treasure of gold and silver, more than enough to fund the construction of his grand temple. Overjoyed and grateful for Lord Shiva's blessings, the king set about building the temple of his dreams.

The temple was magnificent, with intricate carvings and beautiful architecture that drew visitors from far and wide. It became a center of worship and devotion for people from all walks of life, a symbol of the power of faith and the importance of performing religious rituals.

King Chandrasena's devotion to Lord Shiva and his unwavering faith in the power of the yagna had earned him the Lord's blessings and protection. His story continues to inspire devotees of Lord Shiva to this day, reminding them of the power of devotion and the importance of performing religious rituals with sincerity and dedication.

Why do the Hindus wish to visit the Somnath Jyotirlinga once in their lifetime?

The Somnath Jyotirlinga is one of the twelve Jyotirlingas in India, and it holds a significant place in Hindu mythology. It is believed that Lord Shiva appeared in the form of a jyotirlinga (pillar of light) at this location, and since then, it has been considered a holy place by the

Hindus. In this article, we will explore why the Hindus wish to visit the Somnath Jyotirlinga once in their lifetime.

Historical Significance of Somnath Jyotirlinga

The Somnath Jyotirlinga is situated in the Prabhas Kshetra of Gujarat, India, and it is believed to be one of the oldest and most revered temples in India. It has a rich history, dating back to several centuries, and it has been destroyed and rebuilt several times by different rulers.

Legend of Somnath Jyotirlinga

According to Hindu mythology, the Somnath Jyotirlinga is associated with several legends. One such legend is the story of King Bhimdev of Anhilwad, who built the temple to atone for his sins. Another legend states that Lord Krishna himself installed the linga at the site. The most famous legend, however, is the story of Moon God (Chandra) and King Daksha.

Importance of Somnath Jyotirlinga

The Somnath Jyotirlinga holds immense importance for the Hindus, and it is considered one of the holiest sites in India. It is believed that visiting the Somnath Jyotirlinga and offering prayers can cleanse one's soul and lead to salvation. The linga is said to possess immense power, and it is believed that worshipping it can cure various ailments and bring prosperity.

Rituals and Festivals at Somnath Jyotirlinga

The temple follows several rituals and customs, and it attracts thousands of devotees every year. The most famous festival celebrated at the temple is the Maha Shivratri, which is celebrated with great fervor and devotion. The temple also organizes various cultural programs and religious events throughout the year.

Architecture of Somnath Jyotirlinga

The temple is a masterpiece of ancient architecture and engineering. It is built in the Chalukya style of architecture and has intricate carvings and sculptures. The temple complex also houses several smaller temples and shrines, each dedicated to different deities.

How to Reach Somnath Jyotirlinga

The Somnath Jyotirlinga is well-connected by road, rail, and air. The nearest airport is in Diu, which is around 90 km away. The temple is also well-connected by rail, with Veraval being the nearest railway station. Several buses and taxis also ply to the temple from different parts of Gujarat.

Accommodation and Food Options

The temple complex has several dharamshalas and guesthouses that provide comfortable accommodation to the devotees. The temple also has several food stalls that serve delicious vegetarian food to the visitors.

Safety and Security

The temple has round-the-clock security, and CCTV cameras are installed at strategic locations. The temple authorities also provide medical facilities and ambulance services in case of emergencies.

Conclusion

Visiting the Somnath Jyotirlinga is considered a holy pilgrimage by the Hindus, and it holds immense significance in their religious beliefs. The temple has a rich history and is associated with several legends and myths. It is a masterpiece of ancient architecture and engineering and attracts thousands of devotees every year. Visiting

( )

Don't miss out!

Visit the website below and you can sign up to receive emails whenever Rajesh Giri publishes a new book. There's no charge and no obligation.

https://books2read.com/r/B-A-OWRS-VWOGC

BOOKS2READ

Connecting independent readers to independent writers.

Did you love *The Spiritual Journey to Somnath Jyotirlinga*? Then you should read *From Unknown to Unstoppable: The Average Author's Journey to Bestseller Success*[1] by Rajesh Giri!

[2]

Unlock the secrets to becoming a bestselling author with **"From Unknown to Unstoppable: The Average Author's Journey to Bestseller Success."** This comprehensive guide takes aspiring writers on an inspiring journey, revealing the strategies, tools, and mindset needed to turn their writing dreams into reality. Packed with practical advice, real-life examples, and actionable steps, this book is a must-read for anyone hungry for success.

Unique Features:

Inspiring Stories: Dive into the captivating narratives of authors who started from humble beginnings and rose to become literary

---

1. https://books2read.com/u/bQAEQv

2. https://books2read.com/u/bQAEQv

powerhouses. Their stories of perseverance, resilience, and triumph will fuel your motivation and ignite your passion for writing.**Actionable Strategies**: Each chapter is filled with practical tips and techniques that you can implement immediately. From developing a solid writing routine to mastering the art of book marketing, these proven strategies will guide you on your journey to success.**Comprehensive Guidance:** Covering every aspect of the average author's journey, this book leaves no stone unturned. Whether you're struggling with self-doubt, seeking guidance on building an author platform or aiming to hit the bestseller lists, you'll find the answers you need within these pages.**Practical Exercises:** Throughout the book, you'll encounter thought-provoking exercises designed to help you apply the concepts to your own writing. These exercises will deepen your understanding, challenge your thinking, and encourage personal growth as a writer.

Why You Must Read "From Unknown to Unstoppable":
Unlock Your Potential: Discover the hidden potential within you as a writer. This book will help you uncover your unique voice, tap into your creativity, and harness your passion to create compelling stories.**Navigate the Publishing Maze:** The publishing industry can be daunting, but this book provides a roadmap. Learn the differences between traditional and self-publishing, understand the editing process, and gain the knowledge to make informed decisions about your writing career.**Build a Strong Author Platform:** In today's digital age, authors need to establish a strong online presence. This book offers expert advice on building an author platform, utilizing social media effectively, and connecting with readers to grow a loyal fanbase.**Overcome Challenges and Setbacks:** Writing is not without its challenges, but this book equips you with the tools to overcome obstacles. Learn how to deal with rejection, manage self-doubt, and cultivate resilience to stay focused on your goals.**Achieve Bestseller Success:** Whether you dream of topping the bestseller lists or simply want to reach a wider audience, this book provides strategies for achieving success. Learn the secrets of hitting the charts and sustaining long-term success as a bestselling

author.

Plunge into a transformative journey from being unknown to becoming unstoppable. Whether you're a novice writer or an experienced author looking to take your career to new heights, **"From Unknown to Unstoppable: The Average Author's Journey to Bestseller Success"** is your indispensable guide to achieving bestseller success. Start your writing adventure today and unlock the limitless possibilities of your creative potential.

Also by Rajesh Giri

The Spiritual Journey To Jyotirlingas
The Spiritual Journey to Somnath Jyotirlinga

Standalone
Scamming in the Shoe Market: An Inside Look
Still In Love With Her: A Guide To Sustain in a Long-Term Relationship
Beyond Time and Space: A Love That Endures
Love at First Write: Balancing Love and Creativity
Broken Family Stronger Bond: The Power of a Divorced Daughter
Heartstrings: The Art of Loving Someone Who Can't Love You Back
The Phoenix Effect: Rebuilding Your Life After Adversity
Love's Illusion: When Falling Feels Like Flying
Back Bench Lovebirds: A Story of Young Love and Rebellions
Loving My Haters: Finding Strength in Adversity
The Silver Lining of Heartbreak: A Journey to Love
The Mind's Playground: Unlocking Your Potential through Academics
Creating Boundaries with Art: A Guide to Remove Toxic Friends from Your Life
Beyond the Hate: Embracing Love and Forgiveness
Love Through the Ages: The Impact of Famous Love Stories on Modern Relationships

The Winning Edge: Unleashing Your Inner Champion
From Unknown to Unstoppable: The Average Author's Journey to
Bestseller Success

About the Author

Rajesh Kumar Giri is a renowned lecturer of Mathematics, content writer, and a Practical Success Coach. With a passion for writing academic and educational content, Rajesh guides and trains people worldwide, breaking the barriers of language and region with his simple and easy-to-understand writing skills.

Rajesh's journey began in a poor family in a remote area of West Champaran, where he faced numerous challenges in paying for higher education. Despite the obstacles, he persevered and completed his degree, taking his first steps towards educating people and sharing his rags-to-riches ideas. Today, he resides in New Delhi, the capital of India, with his beautiful wife and two lovely sons, and he remains dedicated to serving poor students by providing free education online and offline.

Rajesh has been writing content in the education, affiliate marketing, and health niches since 2006. He believes that experiences speak louder than imaginary and bookish ideas, and his words connect with readers and result in conversions. As a Practical Success Coach, he helps people overcome their limiting beliefs and achieve their goals through practical techniques and strategies.

With his wealth of experience and passion for writing, Rajesh is committed to helping people around the world unlock their full potential and achieve success in all areas of their lives.

www.ingramcontent.com/pod-product-compliance
Lightning Source LLC
Chambersburg PA
CBHW072132150726
48002CB00012B/1446